QUOTABLE LOU

QUOTABLE LOU

The Wit, Wisdom, and Inspiration of
LOU HOLTZ,
College Football's Most Colorful and Engaging Coach

MONTE CARPENTER

TowleHouse Publishing
Nashville, Tennessee

TowleHouse books are distributed by National Book Network (NBN),
4720 Boston Way, Lanham, Maryland 20706.

Library of Congress Cataloging-in-Publication Data

Holtz, Lou.
    Quotable Lou : the wit, wisdom, and inspiration of Lou Holtz, college football's
most colorful and engaging coach / [compiled by] Monte Carpenter.
        p. cm. -- (Potent quotables)
Includes bibliographical references.
    ISBN 1-931249-18-0 (alk. paper)
    1. Holtz, Lou--Quotations. 2. Football coaches--United States--
Quotations. 3. Football--Quotations, maxims, etc. I. Carpenter, Monte, 1956-
II. Title. III. Series.
    GV939.H59 A3 2002
    796.332'092--dc21

                                                                    2002008806

Cover design by Gore Studio, Inc.
Page design by Mike Towle

Printed in the United States of America

1 2 3 4 5 6 — 06 05 04 03 02

To Roger V. and the Czar,
for four years of invaluable mentorship

CONTENTS

ACKNOWLEDGMENTS

LET ME START right where it counts: with all the folks at the Notre Dame Sports Information Department, especially John Heisler and Susan McGonigal. They gave me great access to their Lou Holtz files, press-conference transcripts, and photos covering eleven years. The wealth of information made this book possible.

The sports information departments at William & Mary, North Carolina State University, and the University of Minnesota carved out time to help me with research and/or making Holtz photos available for this book.

The folks at the Nashville Public Library in Nashville, Tennessee, were their usual accommodating selves.

I thank Lou Holtz for being the terrific coach and quote machine that he is, and for his boldness about his Christian faith. Being a true disciple of Jesus Christ doesn't mean keeping it all to yourself.

I thank our Lord, Jesus Christ, for being my Savior; and I thank my wife, Holley, and son, Andrew, for standing with me in the gap.

INTRODUCTION

L OU HOLTZ HAS BEEN one of college football's most successful coaches over the last thirty years, but he doesn't look or sound the part.

Holtz is a wisp of a guy and wears wire-framed glasses. He looks better suited for tending the books at a *Fortune* 500 company than for molding men of muscle and speed into national powerhouse teams. His speech also distinguishes him from his peers. First, there's the lisp. Then, instead of sleep-inducing platitudes and cliché-ish sound bites, we hear the well-chosen words of a polished public speaker, complete with the requisite sense of humor. If he wasn't coaching football, he could be the warm-up act at your local Comedy Corner, perhaps mixing his comedic shtick with a few of the magic tricks he has performed on TV.

When Holtz was introduced in November 1985 as the new football coach at Notre Dame, he was asked how he felt about it. He said, "I'm five-foot-ten, 152 pounds. I wear glasses, speak with a lisp, and have a physique that makes it appear I've been afflicted with beri-beri scurvy most of my life. I ranked

234th in a class of 278 coming out of high school. . . . And here I am a head football coach at Notre Dame."

At Notre Dame Holtz crossed the threshold from being just another good coach with a good record to a nearly great coach with a sustained record of great success. After replacing Gerry Faust, Holtz in 1986 led Notre Dame to a 5-6 mark that was better than it looked. Over the next ten years the Holtz-coached Fighting Irish returned to national prominence, winning one national title (1988), barely missing two others (1989 and 1993), and compiling a 95-24-2 record, averaging just under ten victories a season.

Holtz has worked his turnaround magic at other locales as well, such as at North Carolina State in the early seventies, Minnesota in the mid-eighties, and, now, South Carolina in the early twenty-first century. It hasn't all been smooth sailing, though. His one season in the pros, with the New York Jets in 1976, was a self-described failure, and his seven up-and-then-down seasons at Arkansas ended with a gentle nudge out the door.

If Holtz has worn out a welcome or two along the way, he hasn't lost his touch as someone with an entertaining wit to go with a will to succeed. After taking two years off from coaching to do some television work as a college football analyst, Holtz returned to the sidelines in 1999 at South Carolina.

His first team lost all eleven of its games, although Holtz was distracted much of the year while his wife Beth was battling what would be a successful fight with cancer. Beth and Lou Holtz bounced back in 2000, and the Gamecocks rebounded to post bowl-worthy seasons of 8-4 and 9-3. On the cusp of the 2002 season, Holtz, sixty-five, was the owner of a 233-113-7 career mark.

Holtz can be funny, but he's not all fun. His humor, occasionally self-deprecating, such as when he's discussing his team's prospects for an upcoming opponent, often wears thin. And as quick as he is with a quip in front of a microphone, he has a reputation as a straight-faced taskmaster known to crack the proverbial whip with players and assistant coaches. Even when he's not winning friends, he's influencing people in such a manner that produces success much more than failure.

This compilation of about three hundred of Holtz's quotes represents the best and brightest of what Holtz has said over the years, gleaned from dozens of resources. This is the essential Lou Holtz—at times humorous, at times inspirational, at times brutally honest, and, at times, all of those things together.

QUOTABLE LOU

ACADEMICS

1. Very seldom does an individual flunk anymore. It used to happen all the time when I was in high school. The only way you passed was if you did the work or outgrew the desk.

ACCEPTANCE

2. There are only three things you can do when you have a problem with somebody. Change him, accept him, or divorce yourself from him. Like my wife does something that I just can't stand. She squeezes the toothpaste in the middle of the tube. I can't change her. I'm not going to divorce her. So I accept her. We have two tubes of toothpaste.

ACCOUNTABILITY

3. You choose your friends, you choose your environment, you choose your actions. And you will be held accountable.

AGENTS

4. Let the player go to the NFL team and say, "What's your best offer?" Then take that to an agent and say, "Okay, you get 10 percent of anything you get me above this figure."

—on how players can prevent being victimized by agents

AGING

5. I'd rather have my memories than my youth. I think I can look back and say I'm not as young as I was, but I really like the memories I have.

ARKANSAS

6. Fayetteville isn't the end of the world, but you can see it from there.

7. Every time I could smell the flowers, I began to look around for the coffin.

—referring to a bad season at Arkansas

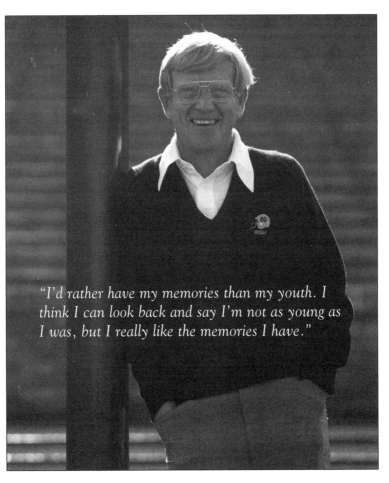

"I'd rather have my memories than my youth. I think I can look back and say I'm not as young as I was, but I really like the memories I have."

8. I'm glad we aren't going to the Gator Bowl.
   —reacting to fans' throwing oranges on the field when the
   Razorbacks earned a bid to the Orange Bowl

9. Nineteen of our best players may not play in this game. I'm sorry to hear this, but I have always encouraged our athletes to think for themselves. If they don't want to represent the University of Arkansas and people in this state against Oklahoma—a team we haven't played in fifty years and the last time we did they beat us, 106-0—that is their prerogative. However, we are going to go play anyway, and we plan on playing well.
   —Holtz's official response to the attorney representing
   Arkansas' three suspended players and claiming that a dozen
   other players would also skip the game in protest.
   The Razorbacks beat Oklahoma, 31-6.

10. Welcome to *The Lou Holtz Show*. Unfortunately, I'm Lou Holtz.
    —opening his weekly TV show at
    Arkansas after losing four of five games

11. It's a bum rap. You hit a nerve when people say I can't recruit. It was never mentioned before I got to Arkansas, where I was also one of the few never mentioned in an investigation of the Southwest Conference.

    —addressing scuttlebutt that he left Arkansas after the 1983 season because of his own recruiting shortcomings

12. You remember I told you about that time I kicked some fellows off the Orange Bowl team in '77. Well, they sued me and the university. But we had a sharp lawyer defending us, and the courts ruled in our favor. Lawyer fellow's name was Bill Clinton.

ARROGANCE

13. When people become successful they think that two things happen. They become invisible. They can do anything with anybody they want and nobody is going to see them. Or they are invincible. They are above the rules and regulations.

ATTITUDE

14. Everything starts with attitude. If you have good teamwork, you're going to have a good product. If you have a good product, you're going to have success. Do it once, do it right. If you have any doubts, get out the Bible.

BETH

15. She has done a great job raising her five children. The fifth is me.

16. It's my anniversary today. My wife and I have been married fifty-two years—twenty-six apiece.

BLOCKING

17. The coaches told me to block Igor "that way." Well, Igor was six-two, 225, had hair on his arms, and Igor didn't want to be blocked "that way." I decided right then and there that if I ever coached, we would block Igor whichever way Igor wanted to go. Then, we'd recruit backs smart enough to run away from Igor.
    —*on his days playing center at Kent State*

18. I have always believed that backs should have to block for one another. . . . I also like for the backs to have to block for the fullback. It just does a lot for team unity.

CHALLENGE

19. Being small and thin, I grew up feeling a little bit insecure, and because of that insecurity, I think I basically had the desire inside to prove something. That may be why I've always accepted challenges.

20. We are always faced with different challenges, and circumstances necessitate bringing out the greatness God puts in all of us.

21. When a difficult task comes your way, accept the challenge joyfully. Once it is finished, plead for more.

CHARACTER

22. If I'm dealing with an individual, do I want him to be on time, to be honest, to be aboveboard, and to give me his undivided attention? I wouldn't want him to be a smart aleck or to give me sarcastic answers or to tell me one story and then tell somebody else a completely different story. I just want my players to be fair, to be honest, and to be aboveboard.

COACHING

23. At a banquet someone introduced me as the best coach in the country. It's true. There are a thousand better coaches in the cities, but I'm the best in the country.

24. Coaching is nothing more than eliminating mistakes before you get fired.

25. The first thing we look for in a house is its resale value.

26. If you can live without coaching, then you ought to get out of it.

27. To coach is to choose, and choosing produces disagreement, dissatisfaction, and conflicts.

28. Don't ever ask a player to do something he doesn't have the ability to do. He'll just question your ability as a coach, not his as an athlete.

29. I try not to ask people things. I tell them. See, I'm the coach.

30. I know I wouldn't want to play for me. I played and coached for guys like me.

31. Football assignments and knowledge always were instinctively easy to me. I can't remember the name of my children or where my socks are, but I can look at film one time and remember assignments.

32. I'm insecure about a lot of things. That may be why I try to make people laugh. But I'm very secure about one thing: my ability to coach football.

33. There's a quote in the Bible that says Joseph died leaning on his staff. The same thing'll be said about me when I pass away.

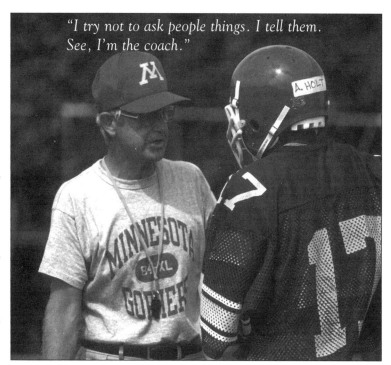

"I try not to ask people things. I tell them. See, I'm the coach."

34. I am a teacher. That's all I am. I don't want to live in a town where the average age is deceased. I want to be around people who have the capacity to dream and learn. I still feel when I'm not coaching, my talents are not used where they apply best. . . . I feel that God wants me to coach.

COLD WEATHER

35. I've always loathed cold. A woman in Arkansas asked me where I was going to live. I said indoors.

COMMITMENT

36. I'm tired of impersonators who put on the uniform but aren't committed.

37. I always tell our athletes, "The qualities you develop now, the things we're going to insist upon, will be with you for life, and they'll always be as sound and as good as they are now." All we're really talking about is a commitment to excellence.

38. When all is said and done, as a rule, more is said than done.

COMMUNICATION

39. To communicate, we must listen. The Good Lord gave us two ears and one mouth so we can listen twice as much as we should talk.

40. My wife Beth and I have a little trouble communicating. When I say "a broad," she thinks about a trip to Europe. When she says "diamond," I think of baseball.

41. One way to save face is to keep the lower part of it shut.

COMPETITION

42. So many times people are afraid of competition, when it should bring out the best in us. We all have talents and abilities, so why be intimidated by other people's skills?

COMPROMISE

43. I have a real shortcoming, and that is I don't compromise real well.

CONDITIONING

44. I told them (players) not to use my physique as a guide.

45. I want to get these guys strong enough to carry me off the field.

COPING

46. If you can simplify life to its simplest forms, breaking down problems to their bare essentials, nothing is really complicated. And even an ordinary mind like mine can cope.

DEFENSE

47. Any time your defense gives up more points than your basketball team, you're in trouble.

48. You are never going to be a great football team until you are outstanding on defense, and being outstanding on defense starts with the ability to stop the run.

DISCIPLINE

49. There is a thin line between discipline and harassment. Discipline breeds success; harassment breeds contempt.

50. Discipline is not what you do to somebody, but what you do for somebody.

51. Everybody says I'm a disciplinarian, but I'm not. A person who won't do what's necessary isn't a bit better than one who can't.

52. When you discipline people, they have a choice to become bitter or better.

DRUGS

53. As coaches, we've got to get rid of pot and drugs—and then we've got to work on Pac-Man.

EAST LIVERPOOL, OHIO (HIS HOMETOWN)

54. It's on the Ohio River, except every spring when it's in the river.

EDUCATION

55. An individual should receive two educations in college. One is an education to teach you to make a living. The other education you receive teaches you how to live.

ENTHUSIASM

56. I go to a wedding, and I want to get married. I go to a play, and I want to be an actor. I get on the airplane, and I want to be the pilot. I get on the bus, and I want to be the bus driver. . . . I go to the funeral home, and I want to be the corpse, too.

EPITAPHS (SUGGESTED)

57. A person who did the best he could in a Christian approach but who failed so many times in the results, but not in the intentions.

58. To my wife—I told you I was sick.

EXCUSES

59. The man who complains about the way the ball bounces is likely the one who dropped it.

FAITH

60. You have to have an ego any time you really want to excel. So I had some problems with that for a while, but I don't anymore. I still stray from it, but I hope that I'll excel for the glory of God. Without him I can't do anything but foul up my life. I want people to know that I have faith in God.

61. God loves you, and you are special.

62. I find that going to confession and to church and reading the Bible makes a person a better Christian. You either get better or get worse in this world as a coach, as a player, . . . and as a Christian as well.

63. I think we all get intrigued with Saint Jude, the saint of the impossible.

University of North Carolina State Sports Information Department

"Nobody is all good or all bad, except Jesus Christ. If there's anyone I want to model myself after it would be Him. But I don't do a very good job at it."

64. Some of us have a foxhole religion. We call on God, we pray when the shells are going overhead; but when the shells stop, we say, "I was only kidding." Our fingers were crossed. Sometimes we pray when the other team is on the three-yard line. I hope I have a better reliance on God because of my faith.

65. Nobody is all good or all bad, except Jesus Christ. If there's anyone I want to model myself after it would be Him. But I don't do a very good job at it.

66. The busier you are, the more important it is to take time to pray. If you only pray when it's convenient, you'll never find time.

67. Football is not my number-one priority. My first priority is my faith in God. Second is my family. Notre Dame is third. My family is far more important than my job. Now these priorities don't usually conflict, but when they do, you have to go with what's most important.

68. There are so many things in this life that are not fair. You work all your life to do something and people try to tear you down. You want to say, "Geez, that's not right," or "That's not fair." But you can't control it or do anything about it. So when you look at the options of criticism, there's really only one option—to pray to God that you have the courage and the strength and won't become bitter and move on with your life. Other than that, I don't know how you would handle it.

69. I don't see how you can live in the public eye and be subject to criticism if you don't have faith.

FAMILY

70. The basis of any society is the strength of the family. This is true in 1989 and, for sure, it will hold true in the year 2089.

71. The qualities that we admire in people—honesty, cheerfulness, thoughtfulness, cooperation—must be learned in the home and developed by society.

72. A house is an address, a home is an environment. And whenever we moved, we always moved a home.

73. A family doesn't necessarily mean you have the same last name or the same address; it means you need one another, help one another, and encourage one another. And that's the purpose of having a family, to love one another unconditionally.

FEELINGS

74. Never be afraid to cry in a time of sorrow. Never be afraid to say, "I love you."

FLEXIBILITY

75. If there is a problem I can't solve, I may have to learn to live with it. Maybe somebody takes long lunches. I don't understand that because I haven't gone to lunch in twenty years. But if that person is valuable, I have to learn to live with his lunches.

FOOTBALL

76. It always amazes me that spectators want to coach, coaches want to officiate, and officials just want to watch the game.

    —speaking at a banquet emceed by a former Big Ten official

77. Football is a lot like life: You start off with needing other people to be successful. You have to subjugate your personal welfare to the group's overall welfare.

78. Football is an educational experience.

79. The average pro career is 3.9 years. Even if you're lucky enough to make the pros, your career is over at age twenty-six. The average life span is seventy-five. So what are you going to do after that (football career)?

FRUGALITY

80. I had a date for the senior prom, but the girl broke it.
    I wasn't too disappointed. It saved me some money.
    —*Holtz on his one date while in high school*

FUMBLES

81. When they put a back in his grave, they ought to be
    able to pry his elbow away from his body and find a
    football somewhere in between.

GAMBLING

82. As a football coach, I have witnessed our football
    players be idolized, praised, and cheered after a win.
    I have also witnessed them being ridiculed,
    demonized, and ostracized after a win. The only
    difference was in one case we covered the point
    spread, in the other we did not. I think that we
    have to do everything we can to remove this
    temptation and to stop the pressure this betting
    places on our young people.
    —*testifying in June 2000 before the U.S. Congress's Committee
    on the Judiciary regarding the Student Athlete Protection Act*

GOALS

83. If you are bored with life, if you don't have a burning desire to get up in the morning to do things, your problem is you do not have goals.

84. Can you imagine walking up to Sir Edmund Hillary after he scaled Mount Everest and asking, "Hey, how did you get here?" What if he said, "I don't know. I went for a walk and here I am"? You have to have goals and dreams, or life isn't very exciting and has no purpose.

85. You can look so far ahead that you forget to do what's required of you now.

86. If you get people to believe in themselves, they'll set bigger goals.

GOLF

87. Golf is one of the few games where the better you are, the fewer chances you get.

88. I used to get real angry over golf. But I learned my lesson in 1974. Playing with a friend. I threw clubs. He told me I wasn't good enough a player to get mad.

89. I've never shot a hole-in-one. The closest I came was once when I got a bogey.

HAPPINESS

90. Probably the happiest I've ever been was when I was an assistant coach at William & Mary College. I didn't make as much money, had more time with my family, and we even belonged to a bridge group. And I love bridge. But I haven't had time to play bridge maybe five times in the last fifteen years.

HEROES

91. One of my favorites has always been Ted Williams. There are many reasons. He was such a great talent and, yet, he developed that talent to the maximum.

HOMEFIELD ADVANTAGE

92. Playing at home is only an advantage if you win. If you lose, you're better off playing on the road, because you have a better chance of getting out of the stadium alive.

HOMEWORK

93. My wife set up an office for me in our house, and I spend all my time there because it is the only place where I am allowed to smoke my pipe. My wife doesn't allow me to do that in any other part of the house.

HUMOR

94. The problem with having a sense of humor is often that people you use it on aren't in a very good mood.

HYPOCRISY

95. A hypocrite is somebody who complains about sex, nudity, and violence on the VCR.

"I think everything should be delegated, so if I went into a coma, the staff could take over."

IDEAS

96. Ideas are funny things: They don't work unless you do.

INSPIRATION

97. We often fail to fully exploit our gifts because we don't realize we have them.

JUGGLING

98. Juggling is something I taught myself to do while I was standing around on golf courses.

LEADERSHIP

99. I think everything should be delegated, so if I went into a coma, the staff could take over.

100. Getting on a player is not necessarily appreciated. But caring about somebody doesn't mean making it easy for them. Caring is helping them to develop their traits and talents.

101. The standards you establish for others must reflect the standards you set for yourself. No one will follow a hypocrite.

102. When you concern yourself with the welfare of others, you engender loyalty and respect. You create value. And you acquire power.

LIFE

103. Life is very simple. Do what's right, do your best, and treat others like you want to be treated. If you follow those three rules, you'll be in pretty good shape.

"THE LIST"

104. I'm a great believer in goal setting. When I was out of a job in '66, I made a list of 107 goals. My wife said, "Add one more—get a job."

  —*referring to the list of 107 things he would like to do in life, which he compiled after losing his assistant coach's job at South Carolina*

LITTLE LOU

105. If I thand in line all thith time and I don't weigh at leatht a hundred pounds, I'm going to be thick.

  —*quote attributed to Holtz when he was a sophomore runt getting ready to weigh in at a 1951 summer football camp*

106. When I made up the list, I was really depressed. I had no idea people would write about it and ask me about it so much.

MAIL

107. If I became a mailman, I wouldn't handle as much mail as I do now.

MINNESOTA

108. Everybody here has blond hair and blue ears.

109. I didn't want to go to Minnesota. I told them their program was in shambles. They had lost seventeen straight games. I said, "Why should I come to Minnesota?" They said, "We've got potential. Nebraska only beat us by ten last year." I didn't know they meant ten touchdowns.

110. We will get the heart and soul of our football team from the state of Minnesota. However, we'll have to go elsewhere for the arms and legs.

111. We should qualify for the United States Football League. It's almost like we're starting from scratch. At least we have offices.

"The players are more optimistic than I am. Heck, people on the Titanic were optimistic."

112. By the seventeenth practice (out of twenty), we'll know whether the fans will have to wear sacks over their heads to the games.

    —on his first spring practice at Minnesota

113. It takes effort, toughness, and willingness to win. We're not asking you to win. When you're ready to win, you will know it.

    *—before his first spring practice
    at the University of Minnesota, April 1984*

114. The players are more optimistic than I am. Heck, people on the *Titanic* were optimistic.

115. I admire the loyalty of Minnesotans. They voted for Mondale, and they keep watching us.

116. I'm worried about the numbers here. I don't know how many colleges play eight-man football. And I'm not real good at coaching that, either.

117. We just hope to make enough money to cover our hospital expenses.

    —*on playing Nebraska*

118. It's the kind of place where your wife cries twice: once when you tell her you're moving there and again when you tell her that you're leaving there.

    —*on the Twin Cities*

119. We had to get and accept a bowl invitation at Minnesota before I would be free to talk to Notre Dame. I would not leave Minnesota until the program was on a firm foundation and moving in the right direction.

120. It was difficult to leave Minnesota, but I'll tell you what would have been more difficult: to say no to Notre Dame.

MOMENTUM

121. Momentum is whatever your attitude determines it to be.

MONEY

122. We had a player (at Notre Dame) named Rocket Ismail. He was so fast he played tennis by himself. He came to me after his junior year and said, "Coach, you told me I'd get a good job offer if I came here. Well, I've got one for eighteen million dollars. What should I do?" I said, "Rocket, I think we should take it."

123. If you make money honestly, spend it judiciously, and are charitable, I don't think you have to apologize for anything.

124. I really only ever wanted two things. First, I never really wanted to be rich. Second, I never really wanted to be poor.

125. Among my many ambitions, I wanted to be a billionaire. Well, I have to say I am independently wealthy. I have enough money to last me the rest of my life—if I die tomorrow.

MOTIVATION

126. I won't accept anything less than the best a player's capable of doing. . . . and he has the right to expect the best that I can do for him and the team.

127. Motivation is nothing more than a sense of purpose.

128. You have to be a self-starter in today's world.

129. I played on some teams that got beat pretty badly, where the other team was frolicking on the other side. It wasn't fun. The pain of losing goes away. The pain of embarrassment lasts longer. Those kind of things happen, and they give you that fervent desire to excel at everything you do.

NAIVETE

130. When my Uncle Lou got back home (from World War II service), he told me the reason the war ended was that the army finally let him fight, and I believed him.

NEW YORK JETS

131. We'll be passing a lot—hopefully to our own people.

132. There wasn't anything I really disliked about professional football. I was not very mature at that stage of my life. The few talents I had weren't geared to professional football. The Jets deserved a better football coach than I was prepared to be at the time.

133. That disappoints me the most in my heart. That still bothers me to this day because I did something that I'd like to think uncharacteristic, walking away from something.

—on resigning from the Jets after a 3-10 start in 1976

134. I was doing everything that I tell salespeople not to do. I gave my word—and didn't keep it. . . . I walked into something I hadn't thought through.

135. I didn't go there (to the Jets) with a commitment. I went to work every day thinking, *Well, if this doesn't work out, I can always go back to college football.*

136. I knew I was in trouble the first day when I tried to call my quarterback, Joe Namath, and was told that I would have to clear the call through Namath's agent.

137. For lunch I have a cheeseburger with ketchup and a Tab, then I go back to my dorm, lie down, and think, *Thank God, I'm in the big time.*

   —*describing life as an NFL coach*

138. (I was) used to an eleven-game schedule, counting the bowl, and all of a sudden you're in a twenty-game schedule. You feel like the season is never going to end. And you feel differently, and you don't always think rationally, and I was doing a disservice to the Jets by remaining there. And, consequently, I did (them) a favor by resigning. I wasn't happy. I wasn't helping them.

OFFENSE

139. To be a solid offensive team, you've got to be able to do five things. You've got to have a power running attack. You've got to be able to run some option. You've got to have a play-action passing game. You've got to be able to throw downfield out of the pocket. And you've got to be able to execute screens, draws, and delays. Our philosophy is to put as much pressure as possible on a defense by forcing it to defend against all those different things in a football game.

140. My philosophy of football is that I don't believe in doing it with Xs and Os. There comes a time— maybe once or twice a season against the great teams—when you have to pull rabbits out of the hat. In other words, you have to gamble because your opponent either is better than you or is doing certain things. But I don't believe you can outsmart people. I believe you win with execution and fundamentals.

"I tell them the offensive line is the last stop before the bus stop."

OFFENSIVE LINE

141. I tell them the offensive line is the last stop before the bus stop.

ONE-UPMANSHIP

142. The following exchange reportedly took place prior to the 1992 Sugar Bowl between Florida and a Notre Dame team with three losses, while Holtz was out dining with his family:

> *Waiter:* "What's the difference between Notre Dame and Cheerios?"
>
> *Holtz:* "I don't know."
>
> *Waiter:* "Cheerios belong in a bowl."
>
> *Holtz:* "What's the difference between Lou Holtz and a golf pro?"
>
> *Waiter:* "I don't know."
>
> *Holtz:* "A golf pro gives tips."

OPTIMISM

143. We built a house our first summer here, and that's a little optimistic for the head coach at Notre Dame. That's like doing a crossword puzzle with a pen.

144. Hey, look, we're gettin' better. Eight guys did the right thing on that play.

145. Most problems are blessings in disguise.

PARTICIPATION

146. The only people who aren't going to be criticized are those who do absolutely nothing.

147. Be a participant in life. Do not be a spectator.

PASS RUSH

148. You have to have four guys take the most direct route to the passer and arrive there in a bad mood.

PATIENCE

149. We have instant coffee, instant tea, and instant restaurants. Everybody looks for a quick fix. There isn't any. You build it day by day. You don't panic.

150. Patience isn't a virtue; it's a necessity.

PEOPLE

151. People today are more fragile than they used to be. They can be broken more easily. They are not just different; they are less secure, more tender.

152. Some persons are like a wheelbarrow; they stand still until they are pushed.

PERCEPTIONS

153. I did a radio show this week, and they asked me, "What do you do all week?" It's true. I only work one day a week.

PERSEVERANCE

154. Don't let failure get you down—Babe Ruth struck out over thirteen hundred times.

PERSPECTIVE

155. The best thing that can ever happen to anyone is to be on top and then have to stand on your tiptoes to touch bottom. Then you can put your life in the proper perspective.

"*Don't let failure get you down—Babe Ruth struck out over thirteen hundred times.*"

156. People talked about our 6:15 A.M. off-season workouts as being difficult and yet that's 11:15 in London. I think everything is relative.

PLAYERS

157. If you can't hug 'em, pat 'em, and brag about 'em, you don't want 'em on the team.

POLLS

158. If the polls were accurate, they wouldn't have to vote every week.

159. I called the NCAA and asked them, now that we were number one, would our touchdowns count seven points? They said no. I asked them if we would get a first down after nine yards and our opponents twelve. They said no. I asked them if there were any differences in being number one and they said, "Only getting asked about it all the time."
    —*referring to the 1988 season, his third at Notre Dame*

160. Anytime you see one of these preseason magazines, you always see Notre Dame ranked in the top twenty because it sells magazines. If we're any good, they put us in the top three. If they think we're going to be decent, we're in the top six. If they think we have a chance to be pretty good, we're in the top ten. If they don't think we're going to be very good, we're in the top fifteen. And if they think we're going to be horrendous, we're somewhere between fifteen and twenty.

161. You don't become number one; it sort of happens. If you sit around and think about being number one, it doesn't happen.

POSITIVE THINKING

162. If you have positive thoughts in your mind, you will be a recipient of positive thoughts.

POTENTIAL

163. I can't believe that God put us on this earth to be ordinary.

PRACTICE

164. I set my watch back and start all over again.

—on handling a bad practice

PREPARATION

165. You always have to prepare for the obstacles that are going to come. Consequently, when they do come, it doesn't affect you mentally near as much as when you're unprepared for them.

166. The time to worry is before you place the bet—not after you spin the wheel.

167. You will
      only succumb
      to stress
      if you are
      ill-prepared.

PRESSURE

168. Notre Dame is like being Arkansas in fifty states. It's not pressure, but there's an awesome responsibility to win football games.

169. Pressure is going to take a big exam when you haven't studied.

170. When you're thirty-five and the bank turned down your request to remortgage the farm, you've got a crop in the field, you've got six hungry youngsters, and your wife ran off with the drummer, you'll understand that there's got to be a resilience to you, some determination, something to get you through tough times.

—on real pressure

PRIORITIES

171. Just decide what you want to do and then ask the
     question, What's important now?

172. If you continually ask yourself, *What's important
     now?*, you won't waste time on the trivial.

PROGRESS

173. We aren't where we want to be, we aren't where we
     ought to be, but, thank goodness, we aren't where
     we used to be.

"THE QUIPPER"

174. Can they pay me by the word?

175. It used to be great to talk without thinking, because
     I've had so much practice. Now I try to weigh
     things.

176. It's great to be at a place (Notre Dame) where you can talk about your faith when asked about it without feeling the American Civil Liberties Union will be asking the next question.

177. I don't try to send a message to anyone in the paper. I don't try to send a message to our squad. I certainly don't try to send a message to my wife. I just try to say how I feel honestly.

178. I'm a little more guarded (at Notre Dame). You can say something that's funny when you hear it, but then you read it and it sounds offensive.

179. I still have my sense of humor. I just hope the alumni keep theirs.

180. I've had one class in speaking and got a C in it. Why would anyone want to hear me speak?

REBUILDING

181. I don't mind starting a season with unknowns. I just don't like finishing a season with a bunch of them.

RECRUITING

182. If I had to choose between speed and intelligence, I'd take intelligence any day. A guy with great speed going the wrong direction is worse than a guy who is slow going the right way.

183. What I'm looking for is a running back who can carry the ball twenty times on Saturday and then show up at practice Monday without a lawyer, doctor, or agent.

"I don't mind starting a season with unknowns. I just don't like finishing a season with a bunch of them."

RESULTS

184. Don't tell me how rocky the sea is. Just bring the gol-darned ship in.

RULES

185. I don't like to have a lot of rules because I can't remember them all.

186. I ask our players to follow three basic rules. Do what is right. Do your very best. Treat others like you'd like to be treated. Those rules answer the three basic questions we ask of every player, and every player asks of us. The questions are: Can I trust you? Are you committed? Do you care about me? People might think this is corny, but I don't care. This is what I believe.

SCHEDULING

187. The days are gone whereby you can build a dynasty. . . . Playing a difficult schedule week in and week out really takes its toll on you physically. Where it hurts you the most is you have difficulty having real productive practices.

SELF-ANALYSIS

188. People think they know me, but they don't have any idea who I am, what I believe, or what is important to me. Or what bothers me and what does not bother me.

189. I would like to be more intelligent, not as impulsive, much more patient, and much smarter, and to have a better memory of names.

190. I'm just a regular guy who has holes in my shoes.

191. I took my flu shot in front of some of the players, and I never flinched. I passed out, but I didn't flinch.

192. My first reaction was that it was the ugliest thing I ever saw, but then I thought it does look like me.
    —*on seeing an $8.95 Lou Holtz doll*

193. My motto has always been, "Ready, fire, aim."

194. People accuse me of trying to downplay our team and build up our opponent each week. I tell our team before the season begins that it serves no purpose for me to go out and say how great they are. If they're any good, no one will have to tell them. I try to be realistic. I'd rather address the problems we have and talk about the things we have to do to become a better football team.

195. We were at a beach one summer, and I had a bathing suit on. My wife looked at me and said, "Boy, you are skinny, aren't you?" I said, "Honey, I'd like to remind you that it was minor defects like this that kept me from getting a better wife."

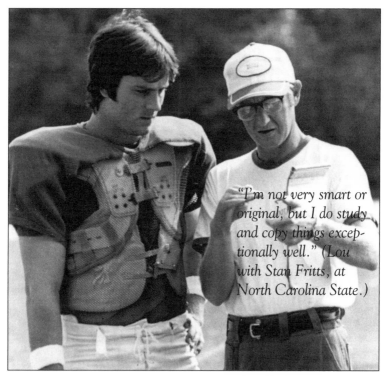

"I'm not very smart or original, but I do study and copy things exceptionally well." (Lou with Stan Fritts, at North Carolina State.)

196. I feel that if I do the best I can in everything, I do think that my life will sort of fall into place.

197. I'm not very smart or original, but I do study and copy things exceptionally well.

198. If I had my way, I'd like for people in the next generation to ask, "What was the name of that lucky coach who won several national championships?" That's how I'd like to be remembered.

199. I'm not a miracle worker, and I'm not a genius.

200. I wasn't a great athlete. I'm not very impressive. I'm not very smart. I'm not very intelligent. . . . Some people are debonair, suave, or great athletes, and their alma maters are maybe going to take them back. My alma mater (Kent State) wouldn't even hire me.

201. I'm so slow it takes me an hour and a half to watch *60 Minutes*.

202. You hear people talk about having an inferiority complex. Me, I didn't have a complex. I was inferior.

203. If I was murdered as soon as practice is over, there would be so many suspects among the players that they wouldn't even try to investigate.

204. What people don't know about me is that I'm a shy person. I'm a private person in a lot of respects, but because of the nature of the coaching profession, you're exposed. A lot is written about you and your life's an open book. Everything, good or bad, is magnified. But I enjoy being by myself and being private.

205. I like myself, and I also think, I know, that I have a lot of areas to improve upon. But in my life I've had one religion and one wife, and I think those are the virtues that have been really important to me.

SELFISHNESS

206. When we are born, the first word out of our mouths after "Mommy" and "Daddy" is "mine." Then you find out the world is not yours, that the world doesn't revolve around you.

SELLING

207. You learn to overcome adversity. You learn to go with the punches. And all that time you maintain a good self-image, and you'll win at sales as sure as you'll win in school or on the field.

208. In a single summer, I sold our car, our TV . . . and not a single cemetery plot.
> —*recalling a summer he spent trying to earn some extra money between seasons as an assistant at William & Mary*

SHOWBOATING

209. Our players don't do dances in the end zone. We like them to act like they've been there before.

SIDELINE PACING

210. A moving target's harder to hit.

SOUTH CAROLINA

211. A lot of people said, "You can't win at South Carolina, and you're making a big mistake if you go there." And they're absolutely right—I can't win here. But our team can, and we plan on doing it.

212. We cannot do it this year. Sometime between now and the third millennium.

—in 1999, discussing South Carolina's prospects for winning the SEC title

213. If I do have a talent, it's my ability to get people to come together and accept their obligations and their responsibilities. If we're going to keep doing the same things we've always done at South Carolina, we're going to get the same results. Players have to change. People have to change.

214. I feel our prayers have been answered. Her attitude is wonderful. I don't pray for her anymore; I pray to her. Sometimes it's harder to live with a saint than to be one. She's getting better every day. We expect to live a long, happy, productive life.

     —*reflecting on his wife Beth's battle with throat cancer, which coincided with his first season (1999) as Gamecocks' coach*

215. This win proves what we can do. Now let's take it to another level. I'm not satisfied, and you shouldn't be either.

     —*on beating Ohio State, 24-7, in the Outback Bowl to complete an 8-4 season his second year at South Carolina*

216. How good are they? It's like trying to tell if a baby is a lawyer or a doctor. I don't know. It's a baby. We're all happy.

     —*appraising his first recruiting class at South Carolina*

STRENGTH TRAINING

217. I think it's important anywhere in college football to have good weight-training facilities. If we win a big game, I'd like to think our players will be strong enough to carry me off the field.

STUPIDITY

218. How do you know what it's like to be stupid if you've never been smart?

SUCCESS

219. Show me a person who is a success, and I'll show you a person who has overcome adversity.

220. If you're patting yourself on the back about what you did yesterday, you haven't done much today.

221. In the successful organization, no detail is too small
to escape close attention.

222. By all aeronautical principles, the bumblebee isn't
supposed to be able to fly. He's too heavy. His body's
the wrong shape. His wings are too short. . . .
Fortunately, he can't read. So he just goes about his
business, flying all over the place.

223. Overachievers are an absolute necessity.

224. Once you accept second place when first is
available, you have a tendency to do it the rest of
your life.

225. I have never heard a successful man or woman get
up and say, "I owe my success to drugs and alcohol."

226. Good things happen to those who refuse to be average and have a positive attitude.

227. No business goes bankrupt if it makes a profit every day.

228. The difference between a champ and a chump is a you.

229. It seems the higher our challenge, the more we concentrate on failure rather than success. I believe we shouldn't concern ourselves with the difficulty of a challenge. Just take a good mental approach to the task and make your best effort on a continuous basis.

230. I can't stand for anyone to lower their standards.

SUPERSTITION

231. The only superstition I have is using a new manila folder every day for practice to make notes about what we need to do.

TEAMWORK

232. The more honor and respect among the team, the greater the team.

233. The greatest thing in the world is to be around people who genuinely care about what you are doing—there's enthusiasm and positiveness.

234. Team rights supersede individual rights. When you walk off that field, you're an individual, and you have individual rights.

"*The greatest thing in the world is to be around people who genuinely care about what you are doing—there's enthusiasm and positiveness.*"

TIES

235. It's true that a tie is like kissing your sister, but that's better than kissing your brother.

TIME MANAGEMENT

236. One of my worries is that I may become a shallow person because of all the time demands. My letters are getting shorter, my conversations more brief. I used to be able to regroup with one day on a golf course—especially if I was having a good day and my partner was having a bad one. I haven't been able to do that much, though.

WILLIAM & MARY

237. We have too many Marys and not enough Williams.

238. We used to play Navy at Marine Corps Stadium in Annapolis. It's a beautiful place, and on the façade of the upper deck they list some of the great battles from history—places like Midway and Guadalcanal and Iwo Jima. We were on the field warming up before the game, and a couple of my players came up to me and said, "Coach, there's no way we can beat these guys." I said, "Why not?" They said, "Well, look at the schedule they play."

WINNING AND LOSING

239. I don't think we can win every game, just the next one.

240. How you respond to the challenge in the second half will determine what you become after the game, whether you are a winner or a loser.

241. The fact that you're $3 million ahead at the gaming table with five minutes left doesn't matter. What matters is, you went in a $20,000 Cadillac and came home in a $200,000 Greyhound.

242. You have heartaches and you have disappointments. Things don't go well and you lose. You don't necessarily have a lot of friends. You have to hire pallbearers for your own funeral. And when you win, you have all kinds of people rejoicing and all of a sudden you find out that's not really what's important in life or in football.

243. Maybe it's the fact that I was brought up in the depression, when you had to nurse a coke for three days because that's all you had. But at the beginning of the week, I really do think schools like Navy and Northwestern look so big and tough we could lose. I'm afraid of losing.

244. There's only one bright side of losing—the phone doesn't ring as much the following week.

245. I think everyone should experience defeat at least once during their career. You learn a lot from it.

WOODY HAYES

246. Woody Hayes was a beautiful person in this respect: He believed in his coaches and players stronger than they believed in themselves.

247. When O.J. Simpson ran eighty yards for a touchdown against Ohio State in the 1969 Rose Bowl game, I was coaching Ohio State's secondary. Fortunately, I was in the press box at the time. But when I got to the locker room, Woody came right at me and took a strategic grasp of my jugular and asked, "Why did O.J. go eighty yards?" I told him, "Because that's all he needed, Coach."

WORK ETHIC

248. I work from dawn to exhaustion. If there's not a crisis, I'll create one.

249. Somebody else said, "What do you do when you go home at night?" I said, "You get about four hours' sleep; the rest of the time you spend preparing for the meeting and the game plan. Your fairy godmother doesn't deliver that under the pillow."

250. Genius: It's 1 percent inspiration and 99 percent perspiration. No one has ever drowned in sweat.

251. The only place you can start at the top is when you're digging a hole.

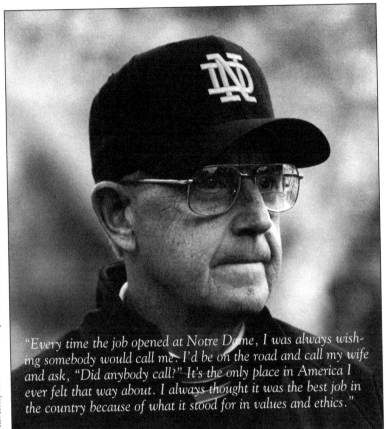

"Every time the job opened at Notre Dame, I was always wishing somebody would call me. I'd be on the road and call my wife and ask, "Did anybody call?" It's the only place in America I ever felt that way about. I always thought it was the best job in the country because of what it stood for in values and ethics."

NOTRE DAME

252. I don't take vacations, and I do absolutely nothing for six months during the course of the football season except coach the University of Notre Dame football team.

253.   I'm not a prognosticator. I bought
       one of the first Edsels that came
       off the market, so I can't really
       tell what the future holds.

       —upon accepting the Notre Dame job in late 1985

254.   Every time the job opened at
       Notre Dame, I was always wishing
       somebody would call me. I'd be
       on the road and call my wife and
       ask, "Did anybody call?" It's the
       only place in America I ever felt
       that way about. I always thought
       it was the best job in the country
       because of what it stood for in
       values and ethics.

255. I didn't come here to change Notre Dame . . . and Notre Dame didn't bring me here to change me.

256. There's a saying here that you don't come to Notre Dame to learn to do something, you come to learn to be somebody.

257. I'm five-foot-ten, 152 pounds. I wear glasses, speak with a lisp, and have a physique that makes it appear I've been afflicted with beri-beri scurvy most of my life. I ranked 234th in a class of 278 coming out of high school. . . . And here I am a head football coach at Notre Dame.

258. My mother is extremely happy these days. She believes that once you go to Notre Dame, you're in heaven.

259. As coach at Notre Dame, what I just want to do is function as the head coach in a quiet, noncontroversial manner.

260. I hope I can display the same type of character and integrity Gerry Faust has in the last five years. I don't think I can recall an individual who has handled himself better in all situations or been a more positive influence in bringing optimism to people who are down and depressed. I don't think we in this room or Gerry himself realize just how many lives he has touched.

261. Our first priority here has been to recruit the athletes we already have.
    —*speaking about his first days on the job, when his first task was to get players to buy into his stricter philosophy*

262. The first thing I did was give the squad a questionnaire that necessitated some essay-type answers. It was the first time I ever had to read the questionnaires with a dictionary.

263. I'm not the owner of the company here. I'm just the caretaker. I'm kind of like a department head of a public-owned company. At most places, the football coach feels like a czar. It's his team, his training table, his athletic dorm. Not at Notre Dame. I'm just here to keep an eye on things for a while.

264. This school will not compromise, and that's not a complaint because I knew that before I came here.

265. I have a lifetime contract. That means I can't be fired in the third quarter if we're ahead and moving the ball.

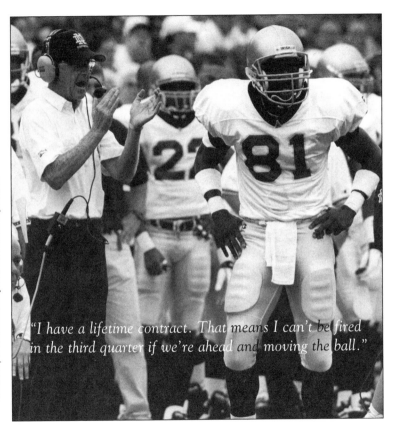

"I have a lifetime contract. That means I can't be fired in the third quarter if we're ahead and moving the ball."

266. No matter where you go in the country, you run into Notre Dame followers, people who just live and die with the program, which makes Notre Dame what it is.

267. We use the tower every day to film, but I am not a tower coach. The thing that I enjoy doing is teaching, coaching, working. I will be very active. I know a lot of people say that you don't have time to do that at Notre Dame; that the demands on your time won't allow you to do it. If I have to stay up until three in the morning to do it, I will be active in coaching. But I won't be in the tower. If you see me up there, it's because my next move will be to jump off.

268. The headgear are solid gold, with no markings, and I thought it would be nice if we put an "ND" or something on them. They let me know that the helmet represents the Golden Dome. When I made my suggestion, they immediately tied my thumbs together until I relinquished the idea.

269. There's no way I'd break out the green jerseys. None whatsoever. Our proper colors are dark blue and gold in honor of Our Lady. I made a promise to myself that the team would not wear anything but the regular school colors.

270. When I was on the outside, you heard about the spirit of Notre Dame. But you didn't believe it. I came here and didn't believe it necessarily. But then I made an interesting observation. If you don't believe in it, you'll never feel it. Then I made up my mind I was going to believe in this spirit. And when you believe it, you feel it.

271. If my faith is as strong as I hope it is, and if it's still growing, it is the only thing that will allow me to cope with the responsibilities and the expectations here at Notre Dame.

272. When they said South Bend, I thought they really meant it. There's nothing south about this.
     —upon encountering a South Bend snowstorm

273. I think it's just a signal that one of the prerequisites to be coach at Notre Dame is that you can't cry.
     —referring to a doctor's visit to
     check out a tear duct that wasn't tearing

274. I'm always real leery of schools that have letter abbreviations. They always seem to be real good. We could be 0-11 and be the twelfth-best team in the country.
     —referring to a tough 1986 schedule that included
     LSU, SMU, and USC in his inaugural season in South Bend

275. The student body here has been the twelfth man. We have a difficult schedule this year. Twelve men might not do it. We might need thirteen.

    —in 1986

276. We tried to get rid of Navy and pick up Oklahoma.

    —joking about the already tough 1986 schedule

277. I didn't come here to be compared. That's the number-one problem here right now. There's too much talk about the coach and not enough about the players.

278. Notre Dame doesn't care for moral victories.

    —after the Irish's opening-season, 24-23 loss to highly ranked Michigan in Holtz's first game as Notre Dame coach in 1986

279. When students at Notre Dame pay their tuition, they believe that entitles them to one national championship during their four years here.

280. Obviously I enjoy being at Notre Dame, but the pressure gets greater each and every year.

281. It seems to me that the boundaries are somewhere between Mars and Pluto. They've gotten players from everywhere.

    —on Notre Dame's recruiting parameters

282. You can sell Notre Dame to a student-athlete, and there are still some out there.

283. We had a jukebox in the lobby, and it had one record—"The Notre Dame Victory March." They played that thing at recess, at noon, and at dismissal. And you've got to remember that, in those years—'46 to '50—Notre Dame never lost. Those were my formative years.

    —on his longtime adoration of Notre Dame, starting when he was in elementary school in East Liverpool, Ohio

284. I was a Notre Dame fan from 1946 when Lujack tackled Doc Blanchard in the open field to preserve a 0-0 tie. My grandfather followed Notre Dame. I followed Ohio State, because it was close to where I lived, but you always followed Notre Dame, too. The nuns wore black armbands when Notre Dame lost.

285. Unless they intercept the snap from center, we'll get the ball to Tim Brown.

     —on his offensive strategy during his
     first season at Notre Dame, 1986

286. If this is supposed to be a rebuilding year, we need urban renewal.

     —after the Irish started the 1986 season
     with four losses in their first five games

287. The Alabama cheerleaders were bigger than our offensive line.

     —explaining a 1986 loss to the Crimson Tide

288. There are a lot of people who say that Notre Dame can't win the national championship again, because of the rule changes, the limitations on scholarships, the difficult schedule we play. But Notre Dame will win the national championship. I just can't tell you when.

     —Notre Dame won the national title the very next season, in 1988.

289. I start off in the morning with my heart sounding like this: Boom and boom and boom and boom. By the time I get to practice, it's like this: Boomaboomaboomaboomaboom. I try to walk to practice, but most times I am running there.

290. Here at Notre Dame they want to make heroes out of everybody instantaneously. You win a couple of games and they want to put you in the hall of fame. You lose a couple of games and they want to say how you are deemphasizing football.

291. I just want to be considered the luckiest guy—the dumbest coach but the luckiest guy—who ever won at Notre Dame.

292. At Notre Dame, you just want to blend in. Enough excitement is going to come your way without your soliciting it.

293. It's the most important thing here. It's never canceled—rain, snow, sleet, or tornado. I do all right until we get to the final thirty-two, then I'm out of my element. I'm all right with those engineering students.

—on Notre Dame's popular campuswide Bookstore Basketball Tournament, in which Holtz frequently participated

294. We're not going to win any games just because we're Notre Dame. We don't want our mouths to write a check that our abilities can't cash.

295. Every place I've been I've had to just about go out and sell the tickets. You don't have to do that here.

296. Notre Dame would survive without football, but our football team at Notre Dame wouldn't survive without the university, and we are just a small part of it.

297. If you preach something long enough, people are going to believe it. Especially in our case, where it's true.

298. I had no idea of the magnitude of the job. And I tell you what, I've changed jobs since I've been here without even moving my family or moving my desk. The job today is far different than the one I took over four years ago.

—in 1989

299. The minute you beat Notre Dame and it isn't a big deal, then I think that we need to examine our program.

300. Players used to want to know if I'd be around for four years. Now I wonder if they'll be around for four years.

301. When I do leave, I hope it will have proven as good an experience for Notre Dame as it was for me.

302. I have no desire to become the all-time-winningest coach at Notre Dame. The record belongs to Knute Rockne or some other coach in the future. I am comfortable leaving here with his record intact, and just to have held the same position as Rockne, Leahy, Parseghian, and others is reward enough for me.

    —*excerpt from Holtz's November 19, 1996, resignation speech*

303. I cannot honestly give you a reason for my resignation, except to say I feel it is the right thing to do. People will say there has to be more to it than this, but believe me, there isn't.

OTHERS
ON LOU

TONY RICE

THERE'S NO QUESTION WHO'S IN CHARGE. HERE'S THIS LITTLE OLD MAN WHO HAS CONTROL OVER ME. . . . HIS VOICE REALLY CARRIES, AND IT CAN SCARE YOU.[1]

—starting quarterback on the 1988 national-title team at Notre Dame

BETH HOLTZ

I ENJOY FOOTBALL AND KNOW ENOUGH ABOUT IT TO KNOW WHAT'S GOING ON, BUT I DON'T WANT TO KNOW ENOUGH ABOUT IT TO BE ABLE TO SECOND-GUESS THE COACH.[2]

BOBBY BOWDEN

HE SEES SOMETHING HE LIKES, AND HE THROWS IT IN THERE. HE'S GIVEN MY TEAM FITS WITH HIS CLEVERNESS.[3]

—long-time Florida State football coach

FRANK BROYLES

HE GETS MORE OUT OF HIS PLAYERS THAN
ANY COACH IN THE COUNTRY. HE'S A
GREAT MOTIVATOR. HE'S A FIREBRAND.
HE'S ACTIVE IN EVERY AREA OF THE
FOOTBALL TEAM; HE DOESN'T DELEGATE
VERY MUCH. HE DOES MORE COACHING
THAN ANY COACH IN AMERICA TODAY,
PARTICULARLY ON OFFENSE.[4]

*—long-time University of Arkansas
athletic director and one of Holtz's former
bosses, who also preceded Holtz as head
football coach for the Razorbacks*

REV. EDMUND P. JOYCE

WE LIKE TO SAY HERE THAT WINNING
FOOTBALL GAMES IS NOT THE PRIMARY
THING FOR A FOOTBALL COACH AT NOTRE
DAME. BUT WE LIKE TO WIN. WHAT YOU
EVENTUALLY REALIZE IS THAT A MAN
CAN HAVE ALL THE GOOD QUALITIES AS A
PERSON THAT GERRY FAUST HAD AND
PERHAPS BE A BETTER COACH THAN
GERRY FAUST. I WOULD HOPE THAT LOU
HOLTZ STANDS JUST AS MUCH FOR THE
RIGHT THINGS AS GERRY FAUST BUT
MIGHT ALSO BE A MUCH BETTER COACH.[5]

*—for many years Notre Dame's
administrator over the school's athletic program*

STEVE BEURLEIN

GETTING UP AT THAT HOUR (FOR 6:15 A.M.
CONDITIONING DRILLS) IS A PAIN. BUT I'LL TELL
YOU ONE THING, SEEING GUYS GETTING SICK
AND THROWING UP REALLY GIVES YOU A
FEELING OF UNITY.[6]

*—Notre Dame's starting quarterback
in 1986, Holtz's first season at the school*

GENE CORRIGAN

WE WANTED SOMEONE WHO WOULD WAKE UP
THE ECHOES.[7]

*—Notre Dame athletic director
at the time of Holtz's hiring*

KEVIN HOLTZ

HE DOESN'T REALLY ACCEPT COMPLIMENTS.[8]

—one of Lou's two sons

MICHAEL VENTRE, JOURNALIST

YOU TAKE NOTRE DAME FOOTBALL COACH HOLTZ, YOU DRESS HIM IN A FLOWERED BONNET AND GINGHAM DRESS, AND YOU HAVE GRANNY FROM *THE BEVERLY HILLBILLIES*.[9]

REV. THEODORE HESBURGH

IF YOU KEEP THE RULES, I WILL GIVE YOU FIVE YEARS. IF YOU EVER CUT CORNERS, YOU WILL BE OUT OF HERE BY MIDNIGHT.[10]

—Notre Dame's longtime president, addressing Holtz upon hiring the coach

PETE CORDELLI

HE IS VERY GOAL-ORIENTED, AND HE HAS A GREAT AWARENESS OF PEOPLE AND SITUATIONS AND HOW TO HANDLE IT. I'VE NEVER SEEN A PERSON REACT ON HIS FEET LIKE HE DOES.[11]

—longtime Holtz assistant coach

TONY RICE

AT FIRST, ALL HIS YELLING IS TOUGH TO TAKE. I
MEAN, YOU LOOK AT THIS LITTLE GUY WHO YOU
COULD BEAT UP SO EASILY AND WONDER WHAT IS
GOING ON. YOU HAVE TO FINALLY UNDERSTAND
NOT TO LISTEN TO HOW HE SAYS IT, BUT WHAT
HE SAYS. ONCE I DID THAT, I COULD HANDLE IT.
HE IS JUST TRYING TO MAKE US BETTER.[12]

GEORGE KELLY

HE'S JUST A VERY PRIVATE MAN WHO IS SO
DEDICATED TO WHAT HE IS DOING THAT HE CAN
SHUT OFF THE OUTSIDE WORLD. HE JUST REFUSES
TO BE UNPREPARED ABOUT ANYTHING, WHETHER
IT'S A GAME OR A SPEECH. HE HATES FREELANCING.
HE JUST REALLY PUNISHES HIMSELF.[13]

*—an assistant coach and later an athletic
administrator at Notre Dame for many years*

NOTES

1. *New Orleans Times-Picayune* article reprinted in *Arkansas Gazette*, July 11, 1980.
2. *Minnesota*, March/April 1984.
3. *Liguorian*, October 1993.
4. *Saint Louis Post-Dispatch*, July 8, 1992.
5. *Michiana Executive Journal*, September 1992.
6. *The Main Event*, December 1987.
7. *Atlanta Journal and Constitution*, December 8, 1985.
8. Ibid.
9. Holtz, Lou, *Winning Every Day*. New York: HarperBusiness, 1998, p. 26.
10. *Orange County Register*, November 28, 1986.
11. *Chicago Tribune*, December 6, 1985.
12. *Selling*, November 1994.
13. *Saint Anthony Messenger*, November 1990.
14. *Boston Herald*, January 16, 1989.
15. *Atlanta Journal and Constitution*, December 8, 1985.
16. *Milwaukee Sentinel*, July 23, 1987.
17. *Chicago Sun-Times*, August 5, 1988.
18. Notre Dame press conference transcripts.

19. *Decision*, February 1985.

20. *Saint Anthony Messenger*, November 1990.

21. Holtz, Lou, *Winning Every Day*. New York: HarperBusiness, 1998, p. 61.

22. *New Covenant*, October 1989.

23. *Minneapolis Star and Tribune*, December 23, 1983.

24. *Saturday Evening Post*, December 1986.

25. *Our Town: Michiana*, October 1986.

26. *South Bend Tribune*, September 6, 1987.

27. *USA Weekend*, September 21-23, 1990.

28. *Fort Lauderdale Sun-Sentinel*, November 11, 1987.

29. *Sports Illustrated*, April 21, 1986.

30. *South Bend Tribune*, September 6, 1987.

31. *Chicago Tribune*, December 6, 1985.

32. *Washington Post*, February 9, 1986.

33. *Los Angeles Times*, November 23, 1988.

34. *Football Digest*, April 1999.

35. *Minnesota*, March/April 1984.

36. *Selling*, November 1994.

37. *South Bend Tribune*, September 6, 1987.

38. *Orange County Register*, November 28, 1986.

39. *Minneapolis Star and Tribune*, November 28, 1985.

40. *Shades Valley Sun*, January 22, 1986.

41. Ibid.

42. *Success Club Magazine*, November 1994.

43. *Chicago Tribune*, December 6, 1985.

44. *Atlanta Journal and Constitution*, December 8, 1985.

45. *Minneapolis Star and Tribune*, November 28, 1985.

46. *National Catholic Register*, November 19, 1989.

47. *Detroit News*, date unknown.

48. Notre Dame press conference transcripts.

49. *Sourcebook*, Fall 1989.

50. *Saint Anthony Messenger*, November 1990.

51. *Wheeling News-Register*, August 17, 1986.

52. *Goshen News*, April 24, 1989.

53. *Detroit News*, date unknown.

54. Ibid.

55. *USA Today*, June 3, 1993.

56. *Rocky Mountain News*, December 24, 1989.

57. *Minnesota*, March/April 1984.

58. *Detroit News*, date unknown.

59. *Orange County Register*, November 28, 1986.

60. *Decision*, February 1985.

61. *Success Club Magazine*, November 1994.

62. *Saint Anthony Messenger*, November 1990.

63. Ibid.

64. *Decision*, February 1985.

65. *National Catholic Register*, November 19, 1989.

66. *Columbia*, November 1995.

67. Ibid.

68. *Michiana Executive Journal*, September 1992.

69. Ibid.

70. *Piatt County Journal-Republican*, May 17, 1989.

71. Ibid.

72. *Liguorian*, October 1993.

73. Ibid.

74. *Notre Dame Magazine*, Summer 1993.

75. *Sourcebook*, Fall 1989.

76. *Goshen News*, April 24, 1989.

77. *National Catholic Register*, November 19, 1989.

78. *Saint Anthony Messenger*, November 1990.

79. *USA Weekend*, September 21-23, 1990.

80. *Indianapolis News*, August 21, 1988.

81. *Atlanta Journal and Constitution*, December 8, 1985.
82. Congressional Record.
83. *Success Club Magazine*, November 1994.
84. Ibid.
85. *Selling*, November 1994.
86. *USA Weekend*, September 21-23, 1990.
87. *Minneapolis Star and Tribune*, December 23, 1983.
88. *Chicago Tribune*, January 16, 1992.
89. *Louisville Courier-Journal*, October 26, 1986.
90. *Michiana Executive Journal*, September 1992.
91. *Minnesota*, March/April 1984.
92. *The Main Event*, December 1987.
93. Notre Dame press conference transcripts.
94. Quotemeonit.com.
95. *Ohio Magazine*, November 1994.
96. *Shades Valley Sun*, January 22, 1986.
97. Holtz, Lou, *Winning Every Day*. New York: HarperBusiness, 1998, p. 172.
98. *Ohio Magazine*, November 1994.
99. *Sourcebook*, Fall 1989.
100. *South Bend Tribune*, September 6, 1987.
101. Holtz, Lou, *Winning Every Day*. New York: HarperBusiness, 1998, p. 156.
102. Ibid., p. 181.
103. *National Catholic Register*, November 19, 1989.
104. *Selling*, November 1994.
105. *Ohio Magazine*, November 1994.
106. *Rocky Mountain News*, October 10, 1989.
107. Source unknown.
108. *Minneapolis Star and Tribune*, November 28, 1985.
109. *Milwaukee Sentinel*, July 23, 1987.
110. *Sports Illustrated*, April 21, 1986.
111. *Minneapolis Star and Tribune*, December 23, 1983.

112. Ibid., November 28, 1985.
113. *Saint Paul Pioneer Press*, April 1, 1984.
114. *Minneapolis Star and Tribune*, December 23, 1983.
115. *Sourcebook*, Fall 1989.
116. *Minnesota*, March/April 1984.
117. *Detroit News*, date unknown.
118. *Minneapolis Star and Tribune*, November 28, 1985.
119. *Milwaukee Sentinel*, July 23, 1987.
120. *Chicago Sun-Times*, November 29, 1985.
121. Holtz, Lou, *Winning Every Day*. New York: HarperBusiness, 1998, p. 18.
122. *Saint Louis Post-Dispatch*, July 8, 1992.
123. *Michiana Executive Journal*, September 1992.
124. *The Main Event*, December 1987.
125. *Milwaukee Sentinel*, July 23, 1987.
126. *Salina Journal*, January 1, 1989.
127. *Saint Anthony Messenger*, November 1990.
128. Lou Holtz-Ohio Valley Hall of Fame website.
129. Ibid.
130. *Ohio Magazine*, November 1994.
131. *Orange County Register*, November 28, 1986.
132. *Minnesota*, March/April 1984.
133. Ibid.
134. *Selling*, November 1994.
135. *New York Times*, November 29, 1988.
136. *Atlanta Journal and Constitution*, December 8, 1985.
137. *New York Times*, November 28, 1985.
138. Ibid., December 9, 1985.
139. Lou Holtz-Ohio Valley Hall of Fame website.
140. Ibid.
141. *The Main Event*, December 1987.
142. *Ohio Magazine*, November 1994.

143. *Philadelphia Enquirer*, November 20, 1987.

144. *Sports Illustrated*, April 21, 1986.

145. Holtz, Lou, *Winning Every Day*. New York: HarperBusiness, 1998, p. 86.

146. *Michiana Executive Journal*, September 1992.

147. Source unknown.

148. *Philadelphia Enquirer*, November 20, 1987.

149. *USA Weekend*, September 21-23, 1990.

150. *Columbia*, November 1995.

151. *Notre Dame Magazine*, Summer 1993.

152. *Shades Valley Sun*, January 22, 1986.

153. *Boston Globe*, November 13, 1993.

154. *Shades Valley Sun*, January 22, 1986.

155. *Phoenix Gazette*, December 16, 1988.

156. *Louisville Courier-Journal*, October 26, 1986.

157. *Sports Illustrated*, April 21, 1986.

158. Gannett News Service, November 2, 1988.

159. *The Sporting News*, November 28, 1988.

160. Lou Holtz-Ohio Valley Hall of Fame website.

161. Ibid.

162. *Success Club Magazine*, November 1994.

163. TCPN website.

164. *New York Times*, November 28, 1895.

165. *South Bend Tribune*, October 19, 1994.

166. *Shades Valley Sun*, January 22, 1986.

167. Holtz, Lou, *Winning Every Day*. New York: HarperBusiness, 1998, p. 64.

168. *Houston Chronicle*, August 15, 1987.

169. Source unknown.

170. Source unknown.

171. *Michiana Executive Journal*, September 1992.

172. Holtz, Lou, *Winning Every Day*. New York: HarperBusiness, 1998, p. 107.

173. *The Sporting News*, November 28, 1988.

174. *Atlanta Journal and Constitution*, December 8, 1985.

175. *Chicago Tribune*, December 6, 1985.

176. Ibid.

177. *Rocky Mountain News*, December 24, 1989.

178. *USA Today*, April 23, 1986.

179. Ibid.

180. *Selling*, November 1994.

181. *Orange County Register*, November 28, 1986.

182. *Louisville Courier-Journal*, October 26, 1986.

183. *Orange County Register*, November 28, 1986.

184. *New Orleans Times-Picayune* article reprinted in *Arkansas Gazette*, July 11, 1980.

185. *Minnesota*, March/April 1984.

186. Lou Holtz-Ohio Valley Hall of Fame website.

187. Notre Dame press conference transcripts.

188. *Rocky Mountain News*, October 12, 1990.

189. *Saint Anthony Messenger*, November 1990.

190. *Minnesota*, March/April 1984.

191. *Chicago Tribune*, November 23, 1988.

192. *Louisville Courier-Journal*, October 26, 1986.

193. Ibid.

194. Lou Holtz-Ohio Valley Hall of Fame website.

195. *Los Angeles Herald-Examiner*, November 25, 1988.

196. *Minnesota*, March/April 1984.

197. *National Catholic Register*, November 19, 1989.

198. *Houston Chronicle*, August 15, 1987.

199. *Sports Illustrated*, April 21, 1986.

200. *New York Times*, December 9, 1985.

201. *Orlando Sentinel*, December 29, 1985.

202. *Los Angeles Times*, November 23, 1988.

203. *The Sporting News*, November 28, 1988.

204. Lou Holtz-Ohio Valley Hall of Fame website.

205. *Boston Globe*, August 22, 1986.

206. *Rocky Mountain News*, October 10, 1989.

207. *Selling*, November 1994.

208. Ibid.

209. *Atlanta Journal and Constitution*, December 8, 1985.

210. *Minnesota*, March/April 1984.

211. *Football Digest*, April 1999.

212. CNN/SI chat channel.

213. *Saint Petersburg Times*, July 30, 1999.

214. *Football Digest*, April 1999.

215. *Sports Illustrated*, August 13, 2001.

216. Ibid.

217. *State Times*, November 21, 1986.

218. *Los Angeles Times*, November 23, 1988.

219. *Goshen News*, April 24, 1989.

220. *Shades Valley Sun*, January 22, 1986.

221. Quotemeonit.com.

222. *Minneapolis Star and Tribune*, August 19, 1984.

223. *USA Weekend*, September 21-23, 1990.

224. *Salina Journal*, January 1, 1989.

225. *Piatt County Journal-Republican*, May 17, 1989.

226. *Goshen News*, April 24, 1989.

227. *Success Club Magazine*, November 1994.

228. *Shades Valley Sun*, January 22, 1986.

229. *Success Club Magazine*, November 1994.

230. *Notre Dame Magazine*, Summer 1993.

231. Lou Holtz-Ohio Valley Hall of Fame website.

232. *Saint Anthony Messenger*, November 1990.

233. *Michiana Executive Journal*, September 1992.

234. *USA Weekend*, September 21-23, 1990.

235. *Los Angeles Times*, November 23, 1988.

236. *South Bend Tribune*, March 3, 1989.

237. *Boston Globe*, August 22, 1986.

238. *Louisville Courier-Journal*, October 26, 1986.

239. *Time*, November 27, 1989.

240. Quotemeonit.com.

241. *Philadelphia Enquirer*, November 20, 1987.

242. Source unknown.

243. *USA Today*, July 28, 1993.

244. *The Main Event*, December 1987.

245. TPCN website.

246. Source unknown.

247. *Los Angeles Times*, November 23, 1988.

248. *Atlanta Journal and Constitution*, December 8, 1985.

249. *The Main Event*, December 1987.

250. Ibid.

251. *New Orleans Times-Picayune* article reprinted in *Arkansas Gazette*, July 11, 1980.

252. *Michiana Executive Journal*, September 1992.

253. *Detroit News*, date unknown.

254. *New York Times*, November 29, 1988.

255. Ibid., December 9, 1985.

256. *USA Today*, June 3, 1993.

257. Ibid., November 29, 1985.

258. *Wheeling News-Register*, August 17, 1986.

259. *New York Times*, December 9, 1985.

260. *South Bend Tribune*, November 28, 1985.

261. *Chicago Tribune*, December 6, 1985.

262. *Columbus Dispatch*, December 8, 1985.

263. Lou Holtz-Ohio Valley Hall of Fame website.

264. *Rocky Mountain News*, October 10, 1989.

265. *USA Today*, April 23, 1986.

266. *The Main Event*, December 1987.

267. *Wheeling News-Register*, August 17, 1986.

268. *Columbus Dispatch*, December 8, 1985.

269. *New Covenant*, October 1989.

270. *Kansas City Star*, November 13, 1988.

271. *New York Times*, December 9, 1985.

272. *Atlanta Journal and Constitution*, December 8, 1985.

273. *Sports Illustrated*, April 21, 1986.

274. Ibid.

275. *Detroit News*, date unknown.

276. Ibid.

277. *Houston Chronicle*, August 15, 1987.

278. *New York Post*, September 15, 1986.

279. Lou Holtz-Ohio Valley Hall of Fame website.

280. Notre Dame press conference transcripts.

281. *Atlanta Journal and Constitution*, December 8, 1985.

282. *Sport*, October 1987.

283. *Philadelphia Enquirer*, September 1, 1986.

284. *Orlando Sentinel*, December 29, 1985.

285. *Philadelphia Enquirer*, September 1, 1986.

286. *Miami Herald*, November 14, 1986.

287. Ibid.

288. *The Main Event*, December 1987.

289. *The Sporting News*, November 28, 1988.

290. *New York Times*, October 23, 1988.

291. *Saint Anthony Messenger*, November 1990.

292. *Louisville Courier-Journal*, October 26, 1986.

293. *Orange County Register*, date unknown.

294. *Houston Chronicle*, August 15, 1987.

295. *Sport*, October 1987.

296. *Saint Anthony Messenger*, November 1990.

297. *Time*, November 27, 1989.

298. *Rocky Mountain News*, December 24, 1989.
299. Notre Dame press conference transcripts.
300. *Chicago Tribune*, January 16, 1992.
301. *Miami Herald*, November 14, 1986.
302. Holtz's resignation speech from Notre Dame, November 19, 1996.
303. Ibid.

OTHERS ON HOLTZ

1. *Los Angeles Times*, November 24, 1988.
2. *South Bend Tribune*, December 21, 1988.
3. *Washington Post*, October 29, 1987.
4. *USA Today*, November 29, 1985.
5. *Washington Post*, February 9, 1986.
6. Ibid.
7. Ibid.
8. *Time*, November 27, 1989.
9. *Ohio Magazine*, November 1994.
10. *Time*, November 27, 1989.
11. *Boston Globe*, August 22, 1986.
12. *The Sporting News*, November 28, 1988.
13. Ibid.